EARLY IN THE MOURNING

Reflections on a Loss Keenly Felt

GERARD BENJAMIN

First published in 2012 by Gerard Benjamin
4/1 Newstead Avenue, Newstead, Queensland, Australia 4006
Telephone: +61 7 3252 2424 • E-mail: ggerardb@bigpond.net.au
www.ggbooks.wordpress.com

National Library of Australia Cataloguing-in-Publication entry

Benjamin, Gerard

Early in the mourning : reflections on a loss, keenly felt /
Gerard Benjamin.

ISBN: 9780977509461 (pbk.)

1. Benjamin, Gerard--Diaries.
2. Grief.
3. Bereavement--Psychological aspects.
4. Death--Psychological aspects.
5. Loss (Psychology)

155.937

Printed by: Lightning Source Australia

Typesetting (in 12/15pt Minion Pro), design and cover:
Gerard Benjamin

Contents

Death is not extinguishing the light;
it is only putting out the lamp
because the dawn has come.

— Rabindranath Tagore

Foreword

GRIEF does not discriminate. All people experience significant losses throughout the life cycle, however the loss of a loved one through bereavement evokes intense emotional pain. It changes our world view and challenges long held assumptions.

Contrary to some ideologies, there is no right or wrong way to grieve. Contemporary approaches to grief do not consider it to be like a bout of the "flu", to which some 'quick fix' remedy might be applied so as to help it enter its 'end stage'. There is now a greater focus on integrating the loss into our lives and continuing bonds with the loved one, as opposed to developing a detachment or 'getting over' the grief.

There is a wealth of literature for professionals about grief theories, approaches and their efficacy. Other books and online websites focus on how to identify grief and suggest strategies for coping with loss. The differentiating feature of this book however, is the personal narrative of Gerard's experience pre and post death of his beloved partner. The book is based on reflections from Gerard's daily journal. It delineates events and associated emotions throughout his journey. The book normalises grief responses and invites the reader to reflect on his or her own reactions.

I was privileged to have worked with Gerard throughout his journey. During our counselling sessions, Gerard exhibited great courage in processing the impact of his partner's death on his life. During our conversations, I was not surprised to discover that Gerard is an accomplished writer and editor having produced a number of published works. Gerard's interest in language and the power of the written word, accompanied by his personal experience of grief, makes his contribution very valuable.

The book is written with sensitivity and pays homage to all who grieve. Gerard writes with a genuine voice and engages the reader with his open, honest approach to what can sometimes be a very private subject. The book will be helpful to patients, families and friends of people with a life-limiting illness or those recently bereaved. The book's brevity will appeal to those whose time or attentiveness is stretched. Furthermore, doctors, nurses, psychologists, counsellors, social workers and other allied health professionals will benefit greatly from viewing grief from a family member's perspective.

Jeanelle Bergin

Introduction

WHEN it's early in your mourning, it seems impossible to imagine that a glorious new day of happiness will ever dawn for you. The weariness and listlessness, not to mention feeling so out of step with the normal world that you wonder if you're not going mad, mark you as a citizen of that strange back country, the state of bereavement.

The journal that I kept during G's gradual progression from illness to eternity, and which I continued during the melancholy weeks afterwards, was not only a factual record of what took place but provided an element of structure during very difficult days. Actually, I am sure that the passage into bereavement often starts before your loved one takes that last breath. All of one's unfolding anxieties about their ailing condition somehow play their part in toughening the emotional muscles, in anticipation of the sad dramatic moment of ultimate loss.

Re-reading that journal has meant the bittersweet experience of re-visiting those tumultuous weeks—G actually comes alive again in its pages—but it makes me feel relieved that I took the trouble, because it is a precious vignette of an incomparable period. It is probably little different from the bereavement journals of countless others, but it is one person's record nonetheless.

G often endorsed the accuracy of something that she had once read: *an emotional response converts an event into an experience.* Even if returning to the agitation of those days has meant a fresh bout of sadness, how rewarding it has been to savour our companionship through such a rare period, rather than simply consign it to a sequence of events that culminated in her demise.

Colliding head-on with the utter mystery of death's having snatched away your loved one is an unparalleled shock to the system. Be assured that what the counsellors tell you is true: things generally get better but admittedly, that's the last thing that means anything when grief has so thoroughly besieged you.

Thinking back to when I have offered condolences to someone who had just lost his or her dearest companion, I realise now that I had no inkling about what that person must have been feeling. The bereavement zone is a private world for its denizens, generally unappreciated by the unbereaved and carefree populace. It's probably better that way because why should more people than necessary labour under grief's inertia. Since bereavement of varying intensities will be pressed upon us all sooner or later, this memoir may offer yet another helpful glimpse into this experience. For anyone in the midst of bereavement at this moment, it might even offer the assurance that no, you're not going mad after all…

Prologue

IT is almost eight months since I last saw G alive. It's a Sunday, the weather is showery and the building's quiet. There are no emails, the phone's silent and I'm wondering why time goes so slowly. There's a magazine article featuring a beautiful photo of G as she sits smiling at her desk. I feel that she's smiling directly at me. I tap it as I pass by, just as I'd tap my iPad. A few weeks ago, I even dreamt that I was about to sit at that very desk to write out some name cards in calligraphy (her usual job), and she said in the dream, "That's my place." I am sure that the dream's message was, "I'm still here and I'm on the job!"

Despite the months since her disappearance, it doesn't stop the momentary surges of anguish. For a while I couldn't trust myself to be in company in case tears came. It's a rarer risk now, but you just never quite know, especially if a particularly perceptive someone looks too deeply into you and says, "What about you? How are you *really* managing?"

I'd like to answer, "I miss her like anything, and there's no one I can talk to who really understands," but I don't, and instead observe the decorum of the moment and reply, "It's a rocky road..." or else the rather more perfunctory response: "OK"—which is what most people are relieved to hear. If, on the other hand, more information is required, I would still keep it brief: "I'm past the stage of being numb, almost through discombobulated, and maybe moving towards philosophical."

Why am I writing this down? It's a precious period and I want it recorded. I don't want to lose the variegated nuances of this painful transition.

On the other hand, there's a competing tendency to toss aside or even trivialise these 'serious' feelings, with the 'sensible' impulse which impatiently says, "Get over it, and get on with your life."

'Hold on a minute,' I remind myself, 'this is a period to cherish, and just because it's uncomfortable and awkward (embarrassing even), don't be too hasty to paper over it. Its poignancy and sharpness will be effaced all too quickly with the passage of time.'

That's why I decided to stay with the journal for a while longer and record what I was experiencing. Now, months down the track, I'm relieved that I did. How often I have saluted someone's presence of mind in having made a feeling and descriptive diary entry.

Decades later, when the description summons up for the reader traces of the original experience, the reader thinks, 'Wasn't it admirable that somebody had the percipience to set down the details of that moment…'

1. Advancing Bereavement

Our spirit... works on from eternity to eternity;
it is like the sun, which though it seems to set
to our mortal eyes, does not really set,
but shines on perpetually.

— Goethe

I am sure that my sense of bereavement began before G breathed her last. You see, apart from her doctors, only she and I knew of her condition. She had always taken the view that not telling family and friends had the profound benefit of sparing them the anxiety-ridden, roller-coaster ride of successive prognoses and medical appointments, tests and treatment. Of course, tremendous inner strength is needed to face all of this virtually alone, supported only by your loved one.

* * *

The last few months of G's life were a strangely profound, lonely, demanding and yet pivotal time of transition. She was more ill than she had ever been, being very tired and quickly exhausted, yet she maintained her spark and quick humour, despite the pain which she must have been feeling but kept to herself. She had relinquished so many of her habitual patterns. For instance, she rarely stayed up long enough to attend to her reading, yet only two weeks before she would have tackled a pile of it. I ceased even raising the subject since she obviously didn't have the stamina or the interest. With extraneous duties at a minimum, I was permitted the luxury of spending more time than ever just with her, whether reading or talking to her, or just holding her.

Once upon a time at the prospect of one of her looming specialist's appointments, I would have been beside myself with apprehension, but there had been such a cascade of anxieties to deal with in the past few years that I had grown more trusting of the Providential Power. It had so far delivered the right outcomes and would obviously continue to do so.

Being her carer has permitted me many lonely moments of contemplating the Big Unknown—still, this has been compensated for by the discovery of more of those latent inner resources which we are told are there for the asking, if only they are summonsed.

It had been comforting to reflect that G and I had been the best thing for each other, and that our energy had been the inspiration for others. When my stamina flagged, I would recite the reflective trio of the 23rd and

91st Psalms and the Lord's Prayer, which somehow put everything back into perspective.

It was strangely paradoxical that the more she needed care, the more she withdrew from living, as the illness took charge. Six weeks from her end, this was very perplexing to me because I didn't know what was ahead. For instance, she might wonder aloud whether there would be a suitable time for her elder daughter to come to her bedside, yet when I tried to clarify her desire, she said to leave it to the planned outing on Christmas Day. In my journal, I reflected: "This time last Friday she was just able to manage a bus journey. Today, she can hardly walk from room to room without my help." In my characteristically optimistic and good-humoured way, I wanted to regard this as just a temporary setback, but a part of me must have suspected that an irreversible decline had begun.

In hindsight, she was really telling me that the end had appeared on her horizon. One day, she momentarily thought that she was on holiday in Buderim where she grew up. "When are we going home?" she asked. In her sleep, she said, "Look who's here…" It's well known that the dying often *see* ancestors who come to welcome them 'home'. Someone told me the sweet story of an old bushman in hospital close to the end, who amazed his visitors when he brightened up and said, "Look, here's my old dog coming to meet me..."

On Christmas morning, G just didn't want to get out of bed. How easy it would have been to ignore this worrying signal and simply snuggle up closer to her. Why shouldn't she be permitted the comfort of her beautiful, light-filled bedroom which she loved so much, with its big windows looking out onto the garden's greenery and the blue of the sky with its passing parade of birds, planes, clouds, rain and stars. Yes, I felt temporarily immobilised by the poignancy of the situation. Why even think of calling an ambulance on this overcast Christmas morning? Why not simply go back to bed and ignore for as long as possible, the fact that G didn't want to arise?

Ultimately, the serious insurmountable fact offered no alternative but to phone G's daughter then the ambulance. This heart-rending decision was only equalled by the dreadful one that I had had to make seven months before—when I called off our long-anticipated United Kingdom holiday at the very last minute. Her condition had fearsomely returned. Instead of a joyous overseas respite, she was faced with further tedious and disturbing consultations and cycles of treatment. Every detail of that first terrible decision is still deeply etched. To cap it off, G asked to be driven to the airport so that she could watch the plane taking off without us…

*   *   *

On Christmas morning, G knew that she'd never return from hospital. In the first two weeks of her hospital stay, I was still planning for when she would return home. I didn't read between the lines when a specialist told me, "She's very sick. She'll be in for a while".

All of the nurses loved her and treated her as a 'little darling'. "Is there anything I can get you, G?" a nurse would ask her. "Just a smile," she'd reply.

I'm sure that they puzzled as to how she could look so pale of body and yet so radiant of spirit. She would hold the hand of the ministering nurse or doctor, as if to console them for the helplessness which they felt. She in turn craved her hand to be held. She told me that she loved my spending each day with her. "I feel wanted," she said.

Amidst her lethargy, she was still as sharp as a tack. "Which is your best hand?" I asked her. "*Better* hand," she replied. "I have only two…"

I was telling G the story of the film *The King's Speech*, explaining how King George VI in his youth developed a stutter which was not helped by his overbearing father.

Later when I was helping G with her meal a little too enthusiastically, she said, "Please slow down, or you'll give me a stutter."

One day she had a very unusual request: "Would you draw a picture of me when I leave hospital so that I know how you'd like me to be, whether young or old, with dark hair, and so on?"

This was just over two weeks before she 'left hospital' for good. I've puzzled over this query and feel that it was her way of saying that she wanted me to find a companion who would be a 'second G' or who would 'carry her soul'. People speak this way more often than you would think. When the death of a venerable family member almost exactly coincides with a birth in the family, sometimes the new baby is said to have the soul of the deceased and is even named after that forebear.

G and I were agreed (with Genesis 2:18) that 'it is not good that the man (woman) should be alone', and that if one of us should survive the other, then a suitable mate should be found. In a prescient moment about five years before, G pointed out a schoolmasterly woman and said, "If anything should happen to me, she'd be right for you."

Months later, I fulfilled G's wish and listed the qualities which I would seek in a companion: faith-filled, faith-full, youthful at heart, intelligent, kind-hearted, spirited, etc. etc. etc. As more virtues came to mind, I added them to the list. Of course the attributes I listed were G's. Ironic, wasn't it? Spelling out the desired qualities of some future companion was a constant reminder of her.

* * *

Later that day I asked G, "Do you mind my coming up to the hospital to see you each day?" She replied, "I love it. I wish that you could live here."

One night on returning home from the hospital, I had gone to bed exhausted, but something had impelled me to arise and send an email update to T in England. The next morning as soon as I had arrived at her bedside, G asked if I had heard from T. I discussed this coincidence with her. Was it G's innate talent or was it a phenomenon of this state? She agreed that she must share some rapport with T. "I always knew that I was on a different wavelength from most others," she said.

That day brought more thoughtful lucidity. "I've been trying to think of what it will be like when I'm not here," she said, "but it's too hard to imagine it."

"You feel sad?" I asked.

"I'm past that," she replied.

"I'll miss you," I said.

At other times, she's full of playfulness, sometimes humorous, sometimes poignant. Her doctor asks her, "Do you feel any pain?"

"Only the pain of loneliness," she answers.

One morning I found her in very good spirits. Next, she asked, "Am I on death row?"

It's possible that the way I answered this question was just how she would reason it to herself. "You've put 100 percent effort into everything that you've ever done," I said, "and one day the poor old body wants to allow the soul to receive a new one. Most people put nothing like 100 percent into their lives…"

She rejoined, "…They want to do it at the end."

I couldn't help thinking that because G has made such an effort all along, she has overflow still to give—in contrast with some in her position who find themselves desperate for the sympathy and reassurance of all around them. As someone observed, the word 'dignity' perfectly summed up how G was dealing with her predicament.

Naturally I tell her about the messages that have come in by phone and email to which I've replied. She asks about a variety of people and whether they had made contact. "Tell so-and-so I miss them," she said.

There were also the insightful asides such as, "You've got to be sick before some people like you…"

It's whimsical to imagine that in a previous life, I must surely have been G's aide-de-camp or amanuensis. During this period, several times she said, "Take a note about this," or "Write a letter to R and D to say how happy I was to meet them, plus ask about A…"

Later that day, G asked, "What happens after death?" This was obviously not the time for deep philosophical or theological discussions, so I offered this answer: "It is said that the soul takes on a new kind of life. People have reported near-death experiences when they've been drawn to the great light, but have been sent back. They say that the light is so attractive that they have no fear of death as a result."

While all of this was going on, the city was in the midst of a once-in-a-half-century flood. It had been raining for weeks and water was being urgently released from the region's dams which were full. Around lunchtime on the day of the deluge's expected peak, all visitors were instructed to leave the hospital for fear that they would be cut off from their homes. Luckily our home was spared any inundation, but there were some frantic hours when I moved as many of our possessions and as much furniture as possible to above waist-height. As it was, the power went off for five days. I kept my mobile phone charged courtesy of the hospital so that I would not be out of contact. Stalwart friends in our building cooked by gas BBQ and provided a meal for me each night after I returned from the hospital, and before I headed to bed by candlelight.

I was only isolated at home for one night and couldn't resume my hospital visiting until the next morning. G told me, "I missed you and felt lonely." Next she asked, "Were we flooded?"

"Not a drop," I answered.

"Thank heaven!" she said. "My reputation is saved." She was alluding to the fact that it was because of her impetus that we had bought our apartment at that spot.

It was merciful that we were spared any flooding or serious inconvenience, unlike many parts of the city and the state. For several days, G's daughters and son found it impossible to reach the hospital because of the traffic holdups and detours caused by the ongoing emergency.

G's chief doctor and his assistant ask whether our home is safe from floodwaters. The doctor explains to his colleague about the book which G and I wrote, particularly the chapter describing a famous medical dynasty, descendants of which work in this very hospital. It is obvious that both doctors have a tremendous respect for their patient.

Later G said, "They thought I was going to die this month…" "…but you intend to pull a bunny out of the hat, don't you?" I replied, to which she nodded. So many times in her life, G had proven to have the 'bounce-back' resilience of a cork.

The next morning, G said, "I died three times last night."

"You're like Lazarus," I replied. "You came back to life."

Little did I know that she was less than nine days out from doing a non-Lazarus. She wanted me to record the fact that she had brought three babies home from this hospital. It is only as I write this that I realise how poetic was her insistence about those three births, as if to balance up the 'three deaths'.

Afterwards she said, "Will I be alive at Christmas?"

We calculated that this was eleven months away, so I said, "Why not?" That same day, she wrote in a notebook (her once superlative writing becoming hard to decipher), "You're more liked than I am…" I replied, "We're a team. They get both of us." I motioned towards X, the voluble lady sharing G's room who was in far better health. "Even though X makes more demands upon the staff, they are intrigued about what you *don't* say. You and I have a connection which they can't fathom. That's what they really like…" This time G wrote, "I need to write a book about the psychology of all of this."

At lunchtime that day, G seemed a little distressed and didn't want me to leave her. "I might die soon," she said. The next day she was calmer. She refers to me as 'my Gerry.'

A week before her passing, she said, "Tell Dad that I've got A's name." Her voice is very weak and I have to put my ear close to her mouth. Though I didn't understand what she was trying to say, this assumption that she was with her long-dead father is apparently a characteristic of those close to the end. A little later she said, "When I die, the flowers are to go to Mum in Buderim, and she can give them to all the people there…"

'Typical G,' I thought, 'as practical as ever.' How much more sombre would these words have made me, if I had known how short her time was. Some might discount these presentiments as simply the medication speaking, but surely even then they're communicating something from the rich wellspring of an individual's unique subconscious.

G had been at the hospital for almost four weeks and now steps were in train to settle her in a hospice. The day before the anticipated move, she seemed uneasy and I sat for quite a while just holding her hand.

At times there were messages that she wanted to convey, but the sentences would peter out. She still picks up her pen with alacrity and does her best to form beautiful letters. A nurse from Zimbabwe felt her hands and said, "How smooth they are, G. You have not done hard labour in your life." G indicates the pen. The nurse understands, "Ah, you have done hard labour with your pen…"

That night I dreamed of G and the lines from the Dylan Thomas poem: *Do not go gentle into that good night/ Rage, rage against the dying of the light.*

Well, G certainly wasn't going quietly. If anything, just as the poem suggested, she continued glowing in spirit despite encroaching darkness. When a nurse announced, "They are coming for you this morning," (meaning the ambulance staff to transport her to the hospice), G said, "You mean the hearse?"

At this time the most persistent question that G was asked related to how she was managing with any pain. Nurse Emma (who had particularly warmed to G) asked her, "Do you have pain anywhere at the moment?" G answered, "In my heart." There was a pause, then G added, "Do you have a pain in your heart?" The nurse gulped as if G had looked right inside her, then hesitated, before weighing up her professional responsibility and her desire to respond to what G had obviously perceived. What an uncanny ability she had to see how people really are. No wonder the staff were sorry to see G being moved from the hospital.

* * *

I arrived at the hospice 30 minutes before G and was impressed with its calm dignity and the room's homeliness. When G was wheeled in, she looked around and said, "I could live here."

The next morning, the hospice doctor took me aside and said, "When I first saw her, my immediate reaction was that she's close. It will be days and weeks, rather than longer." It proved to be days only…

Tucked in beside her was a little cuddly bear with its purple bed-cap (G's favourite colour), a gift from her second daughter who had christened it 'Vincent' after the name of the hospice. The staff were good-humoured. "We'll need you to bring a change of nightgown for G," one said to us. "Do you have a change of clothing for her little bear?"

When stamina permits, G is full of fun when her children and grandchildren are with her. Her youngest grandchildren may have been taken aback at first to see how ill their Grandma was, but they are likely to remember her as summoning all of her joviality for their visits, as well as for her other well-wishers. Some may have felt very distressed to learn of her advanced condition so late in the day, but this has to be balanced against the heartache which she spared them.

G is on medication which has her asleep most of the time now. She sometimes holds my hand and gives it a squeeze. The nurse explains that this is how it is likely to be from here on in, because of her need for more pain relief. As I wrote at the time, "This is why I've been recording this journal, because the day will come when there's no more to record…"

The next morning, G was much more with it. She gave me a hug and knew it was me—but she's very pale, her nose is cold, and her breathing very laboured, with its long pauses then deep gulps. For some reason, I thought of those lines from Adam Lindsay Gordon, the much-loved poet whom, G told me, her grandmother Agnes Neil oft-quoted: *Two things stand like stone; Kindness in another's trouble, courage in your own.*

This could have been the mantra by which G lived her life. She was the epitome of those sentiments in the 31 years I had known her. The day before she passed away, they moved G to her own room. It had a beautiful view, and there, just over a kilometre away, between tall buildings and to the right of the city's landmark bridge, I could glimpse the spot once occupied by the small private maternity hospital where she had been born 81 years before. There has to be something divine about that sort of symmetry.

Sometimes there's a sleepy sigh, as if she is trying to say something. A visitor, just returned from overseas, had brought us a book of A.E. Housman's poetry. As I recited it to G, sometimes she would offer a sing-songy response as if, despite her drowsiness, she were signalling her appreciation. One line summed up her life to a tee: *Through [her], the gale of life blew high*—but now it had almost run its course.

In my journal later that afternoon, I observed, "It's as if she's already gone, yet still breathing." I noticed that several pages in her medical file had been stamped in red with the word "ceased", obviously referring to medication. 'Cease' means to come to an end. Should 'de-cease' mean the opposite of coming to an end? I left her bedside late on that Sunday afternoon to return home. She had more colour in her cheeks and I wondered if she didn't look better than yesterday.

2. *The day I'll never forget*

[She] was my North, my South, my East and West,
My working week and my Sunday rest,
My noon, my midnight, my talk, my song;
— W.H. Auden

NOTHING quite prepares you for that dreaded phone call at 1.10 on a Monday morning. Instantly wide awake, I steeled myself as the nurse said, in a measured but slightly distressed voice, "I regret to tell you that G passed away 30 minutes ago without warning." Subconsciously, I am sure that I was ready for it, but it still brought a little shock when the ultimate moment arrived. Seven hours before, I had kissed her goodbye, wondering if it really would be farewell—but thinking that it wouldn't be, because she seemed to have rallied. Two days earlier I had been almost too afraid to go to lunch in case she slipped away…

As I put the phone down, there was no paroxysm of tears. Isn't the mind wonderful how it can switch to duty mode and simply get on with making the middle-of-the-night phone call to alert the family relay. Next, it's the drive through the darkened city streets, arriving at the hospice, looking up at the not-quite-darkened window of her room, buzzing the intercom at the front entrance, and finally making my way into where she lay, asleep to the world for eternity. Tucked in beside her was the cuddly bear. How sweet was the staff member, whoever she was, who had made sure that G had her cosy little mate for her celestial jaunt.

I sat with her, running my hand over her blessed, still-warm brow and holding her hand, trying to preserve its diminishing warmth. Oh, what a mystery is death! Had it been the day before, her eyes would have opened from her slumber, given a twinkle of recognition, accompanied by the almost imperceptible smile on the lips, before drifting back to sleep. The nurse had said, "Take all the time you need," though she was surprised that I was still there two hours later. We both knew that it was time to part. Quietly I collected G's few belongings. She lay facing the window, as if looking in the direction of her ultimate escape. Vincent was still tucked in contentedly beside her so I was happy to leave her cuddlesome companion with her, but the nurse said, "You'd better take him." I anointed G's forehead, recited the 23rd Psalm, and kissed her for the last time—reassured that her immense spirit could never be diminished by something as trifling as the wearing out of her body.

That first day, I discharged my duties (G would no doubt say 'admirably') but there were moments when I found myself wandering around not sure of what to do next. Sometimes, there would be an unexpected meteor shower of tears but I was too busy to let it debilitate me.

Helped by her three children, I managed the arrangements, wrote the eulogy and produced the orders of service. During the farewell ceremony, when someone edged a box of tissues towards me along the pew just before I was due to read the eulogy, I remember thinking somewhat dismissively, 'Why would I need them?' Instead, I seem to have been carried along on a wave and was the epitome of 'mine host'. I cheerily greeted attendees at the church and did my best to add levity to the weight of the condolences offered me at the morning tea afterwards.

3. After the Farewell

The weight of this sad time we must obey,
Speak what we feel, not what we ought to say.
— Shakespeare

RETURNING alone to the empty apartment after the funeral brought the first sledgehammer blow that G had really gone. This time last week, she was alive and I had a purpose and structure to my life. I had no interest in eating much, I perfunctorily leafed through the newspaper without seeing the pages, the computer was silent and television held no interest.

For the past few weeks, Saturday evenings had been spent at the hospital. Even thinking of the hospital brought me to the verge of tears. Surely in twelve months, things will look better. Right now, perhaps the best policy is to make a timetable to visit friends in order to provide the people contact that I find myself craving as a substitute for my mate. On the other hand, no matter how often I fill up my time with seeing other people, I still have to come home and face the empty house, all alone.

The day after the funeral brought no relief. I could hardly forestall a whimper starting at every turn. Absolutely everything reminded me of her. In a way, it's hard to see how life will ever return to any normality. Even if I endeavour to be out with people, I'm likely to start to blubber.

I delivered two roses from G's funeral bouquet to a neighbour this morning and it was a relief not to be invited in. How many lonely hours did G and I spend in the last six months, as she became progressively more ill? How very gloomy she must have felt, with no one knowing or understanding. How she craved the input that thoughtful people offered, but she had just me for company hour upon hour. How did she manage to be so calm, knowing that mortality was marching her way?

I find myself faced with the conundrum: is it better to go out and busy myself, or is it wiser to stick with the isolation, in the hope that bereavement, when confined, more quickly loses its sting?

Out of the blue comes an invitation to dine with friends. It's like manna from heaven! Despite my trepidation, it proves to be a pleasing outing and a welcome break from the bereavement zone. Perhaps it is a more sensible policy to ensure that there's some people contact every day…

Even after a week, the home is heavy with the scent of a particular bouquet of flowers from her farewell service. I'm sure that I'll always associate its scent with this event.

Trying to restore some order to the house—it had been sorely neglected for weeks and weeks—I begin sorting through a drawer of G's papers, especially all the medical correspondence and hospital notes. I re-discover a prognosis following her big operation almost three years before: "50% chance of a five-year survival". If that meant that she had two-and-a-half years to live after the operation, then she managed to give us another three months. No wonder the tears start again, as I re-visit in my mind the arduous medical trail which she trekked week after week, ever aware of the ultimate destination.

I have heard that some people retreat to bed in the hope that bereavement will pass. I faithfully arose each morning, thankful for the traditional duties of this period. I mailed out more than 100 'Return Thanks' cards with a personalised message for each recipient. It was time-consuming, yet I considered it to be a recuperative milestone when it was completed. I also individually answered an avalanche of condolence emails. Because so many of them were heartfelt and eloquent tributes to G which it would be a tragedy to lose, I compiled them into a little printed booklet, complete with colour photos. These I distributed to family members and some friends, as an enduring memento.

Needless to say, these exercises induced many abruptly poignant moments, when it was better to cease proceedings and rest awhile in that recollective state. I am sure that these rituals, as the counsellor called them, helped to smooth some bumps out of the bereavement bridleway.

A week after the funeral, I began sorting through another portion of G's papers, trying to decide what to save and what to discard. That alone is a bittersweet task of reminiscence and sadness. With one package completed, I closed the drawer but it wouldn't quite go into place. It was only a matter of a few millimetres, but something was jamming it. What is it about the early bereavement period that sees you on the one hand, beset by a general lassitude, but on the other, pernickety to the point of obsession in trying to impose order? I removed the whole drawer and reached behind in search of the obstruction. Out came a small psychology book which had been tightly wedged in behind the drawer. It had been missing for about two years! G and

I had racked our brains for its whereabouts and had turned the house upside down in its quest. Here it was! I felt like jumping for joy and running to find G to say, "Guess what I've just found!"—but then like a frigid drenching, once more I'm faced with the grim reality. I say to G in my heart, "Thanks for finding it", because to my mind she's still here…

4. Counselling

For my sake, turn again to life and smile,
Nerving thy heart and trembling hand to do
Something to comfort weaker hearts than thine.
Complete those dear unfinished tasks of mine,
And I perchance, may therein comfort you.

— A. Price Hughes & Mary Lee Hall

BOTH the hospital and the hospice sent condolences and offered free counselling if desired. 'Of course, I don't need counselling,' was my immediate reaction. Two months after G's passing, I decided that maybe I shouldn't have been so hasty. Perhaps I could learn something. I made an appointment with the hospice, and even typed out a summary of discussion points in true teacher style, clearly showing how 'on-top' of the situation I was.

The counsellor was skilled and compassionate. I had just explained that while I hadn't experienced the opening of the floodgates, I did find that tears were liable to appear at the oddest moments; indeed several weeks before, I had truly felt worried about being in company, in case I started to feel weepy, but now considered that

I was well past that stage. By the counsellor's second question, I found myself clutching a handkerchief as I fought to hold back a tearful torrent. How quickly she lifted the lid on the wellspring of grief which I thought I was managing quite OK.

"Tell me what your life is like without G," said the counsellor gently.

"To put it in a nutshell," I answered, "I'm still getting used to the missing crew-member beside me on the flight deck, but I'm weathering the turbulence and maintaining our original heading." This unusual vignette occurred to me out of the blue one day. It was apposite since I had once held a pilot's licence and we both loved travelling.

"You're not going to crash?" asked the counsellor. She was checking whether I had been so subsumed with despair that life was no longer worth living.

"No," I answered. "I really do plan to maintain our heading. To continue doing the work which we always did together, would be one way of honouring her. I shared my whole life with G and we discussed everything. I must admit that sometimes my energy wilts, and I feel caught in mid-air with almost no lift under my wings…"

"For some people, what you're going through often causes their whole world to fall apart, and that includes their religious beliefs," said the counsellor. "What are your beliefs and has G's passing challenged them?"

I explained that both of us shared a Christian faith which wasn't of the church-going variety, and no, G's loss hadn't overturned my spiritual applecart. On the other hand, this didn't make her going any easier to explain.

"As a Christian," I said, "I've been taught that life is eternal. G was someone who seemed to come pre-loaded with a wise benevolence. I can't believe that a spirit as fine as hers just ceases to exist. I'm sure that it lives on. I'm sure that this is all part of a divinely providential jigsaw…"

This was theological territory which I knew the counsellor could not comment upon, but it seemed terribly important to explain to her what sort of person G was.

"She was interested in putting spiritual and psychological ideas into practice herself, and she was a first-rate teacher. She inspired many people, young and old," I said.

The counsellor was clearly testing whether anger was rumbling my innards, because why wouldn't some people want to fulminate against the vicissitudes of cruel fate and ask, "Why her and not me? Why now?"

I have no answer to questions such as these and I'm sure that none is expected. It's my nature to look for the silver lining in what happens in life, rather than to rail against its seeming injustices. Call it a philosophical approach if you like, but I salute G for her graceful and dignified exit. She would never have wanted to be debilitated or to become a long-term burden on anyone. If it's possible to say that amidst a serious illness, a person chooses their moment to resign from this life, then top marks to G for the composure with which she slipped away.

The counsellor assured me that if I didn't want to make the effort to see others or to participate in everyday matters in the way that I normally would, it was more sensible to be kind to myself for protection's sake and say no. "Don't put yourself under obligations which stretch your resources," she said. "If you have no overflow to offer, then don't offer, and have no qualms about what others may think. Protecting yourself is a priority when you're in this state."

This advice was more than vindicated when an elderly fellow who had lost his wife years before, asked how I was managing, before explaining to me: "I went to a friend's funeral the other day and shouldn't have gone. I realised how upset I was still feeling for my own loss. Sometimes it's better to say no."

*   *   *

"How long does bereavement last?" I asked the counsellor. I was thinking of a day when I must have looked particularly bereft. A sagely matriarch sidled up to me and advised, "Be sure to give yourself a year before you make any important decisions."

"The time varies from person to person," answered the counsellor.

I was generally aware of my vulnerability (from the Latin: 'wounded'). It's possibly providential and merciful that one feels too listless and dejected to undertake any profound commitments, let alone rash ones. Looking back on the early months of mourning, I can say with relief, "There but for the grace of God went I." Months later, I saw a Harvard study which quantified the wisdom of the woman's advice. Two groups of volunteers were wired up for physiological monitoring so that their biometrical readings could be taken. Members of the first group were shown a decorative object and were asked how much they would pay for it. The second group was also asked, but only after watching a portion of a sad video, during which their biometric readings noticeably declined. This 'sad' group, on average, opted to pay *four times more* for the item than the other group.

In other words, when one's spirit is below par, things risk being seriously over-valued as part of an unconscious mechanism to restore one's equilibrium. What a cautionary example of how the extreme sadness of the bereaved state is capable of distorting one's judgement.

* * *

When the counsellor spoke of the 'first time syndrome', I could offer plenty of examples, such as attending a history society meeting a month after G's passing. It was held adjacent to where her farewell service had taken place. At the last minute, I almost turned on my heels and darted away. Instead I forced myself to go through the motions of signing in, trying to smile at people, making stilted conversation and quickly finding a relatively obscure seat at the back. A kindly woman next to me simply touched my arm which said it all. Of course, it wasn't as bad as I imagined and instead I felt rewarded by people's kindness and compassion. I'm glad that I made the effort because it was much easier the next time.

As the counsellor pointed out, bereavement is a tricky path. Sometimes it's imperative to protect oneself, while at other times, it's worth gently pushing the boundary so as to come to grips with the new reality.

By contrast, it was too distressing by far to go anywhere near the pathology clinic where G ended up being a frequent and much-welcomed attendee. The staff loved her quick wit and stimulating conversation, yet professionally they had known for years what she was facing. Six months after G's last visit, I had no choice but to attend on my own behalf. The staff member, though she was managing a full waiting room, came around to my side of the counter and gave me a hug. That really touched something. Later she asked how I was managing. Up came the lump in the throat and that little stab of tears at the back of the eyes. I managed to say, "I'm doing OK."

"I suppose there are so many reminders of her everywhere," she replied, stating the obvious but doing her best.

As soon as I could, I stammered goodbye, kept my head down so that no-one else might be tempted to say hello and hurried away. Even when people express their feelings out of genuine compassion, it's a double-edged sword because it's just another way of highlighting, emphasising and underlining the fact that as far as the big wide world is concerned, G is *gone for good*. In such moments, I realised just how terribly bruised I feel…

* * *

"Tell me about your happiest times together," the counsellor said, so I explained to her the acute sense of contentment which I felt when G was quietly reading the newspaper just a metre from where I was doing my computer work, even if not a word were spoken.

G relished devouring the daily newspaper when it arrived. It was one of the simple domestic rituals in the home. Equipped with a red pen to mark something interesting, a pair of scissors to cut out an article if necessary, and a bulldog clip for holding the cuttings which she judged I might find interesting, she would devote herself to the task. Later we would talk about what she had found. There came the stage when G said, "I'm a little tired at the moment. I'll just have a short rest before I read the newspaper." They would remain unread for lengthening hours each week. A week's worth would mount up. Although she would make a determined effort to get through them all, eventually it was with a heavy heart that I committed the pile, unread, to the rubbish bin. She was withdrawing from life…

"The same happened with our morning walks which we had enjoyed together for years," I told the counsellor. "In the latter months, these walks progressively became shorter and decreased to every other day, then once a week, and eventually they were beyond her. There was a morning when I walked alone and in one of those heart-rending realisations, I knew that a line had been crossed. Gone forever were our ambles together…"

* * *

"Tell me when you miss her the most," asked the counsellor, so I explained that we often joked that in years to come, doctors would review your blood tests, weight and blood pressure, and also ask, "How's your cuddle-count? You *are* getting enough cuddles, aren't you?"

"What I miss most is having her near to me all day," I answered.

Some people have a tremendous need for physical closeness. G must have had a koala bear's worth of the cuddlesome gene. I'm sure that the soothing touch of a warm and loving companion is not just happiness-engendering but health-enhancing as well. Needless to say, bereavement brings a dearth of touching. Suddenly, the casual hug or the peck on the cheek becomes critically important. I had taken for granted just how much touch there was between G and me each day. All of that was gone.

I amuse myself with the whimsical thought that during the first months, I could easily have set myself up at a street market with a sign: "Hand-holding Here. FREE! Make it as long as you like." How many poor devils are there who haven't had their hand held for weeks, perhaps for years?

As someone perceptively observed, there's only one thing worse than talking about the loss of someone so close, and that's *not* being able to talk about it. What a balm it was just to express how I felt and what G meant to me, and how much I missed her.

I had planned to make the third one-hour session my last because I felt that I had taken up enough of the counsellor's time, but was amazed during that session when she deftly elicited the fact that the sense of isolation that I was feeling now, probably had its resonance with earlier periods in my life when I also felt very sad. I thought a lot about this and concluded that rather than feel that I had somehow 'regressed' as a result of G's passing, it was truer to picture it as another 'isolation quadrant' on the upward spiral of my life's journey. I might be travelling through a rough patch now, but surely just as I had endured earlier tough periods and emerged stronger, so too would I manage this time.

By the end of the fourth session, we both knew that the meetings had served their purpose and that it was a matter of my soldiering-on solo along bereavement's rocky path. I gathered that I was faring OK. For some people, the path is so tortuous that just staying alive is considered an achievement. How fortunate I felt for this opportunity. Bereavement is such foreign territory that it would be foolish to spurn any helping hand that's offered.

5. Dreams &
Ultimate Questions

Those who love deeply, never grow old.
They may die of old age,
but they die young.   — A.W. Pinero

AT the hospice, a senior doctor beckoned me aside for a quiet word. "When the time comes," she said, "shed your tears for G. Don't be afraid to express your sorrow. Some people try to drown it in drink or escape it with travel or crowd it out with frenetic activity. Hang in there as you go through the torment of grief, and you'll emerge stronger for having faced it."

Intuitively, I knew that she was right and I offered no resistance to the strange confinement that bereavement brings. Thinking that I probably needed to get out more, a compassionate friend asked if I would like to attend meditation sessions at the local church. Considering that bereavement seemed to induce an almost constant ruminative state—which may have looked like being lost in thought, but was really a kind of trying to find light in the deepest parts of oneself—I was appreciative for the thoughtful offer but declined. Very likely the bereft state seeks to accomplish exactly what meditation is aiming to bring about: finding and isolating the important thoughts, discarding the distractions, and doing one's best to discern the practical steps forward. It came as a surprise when someone told me that they had ridden past me on their bike when I was out walking. "I would have stopped to talk, but you seemed to be in your own world. I didn't want to intrude," the person said.

Naturally, I dreamed of G after her passing. One scene was particularly vivid:

I was with G on the verandah of a hilltop house. A woman, a bookseller from long ago, asked to speak to G, so I said that I would call her. Just then, I remembered that G had died, so I felt embarrassed and upset about having to explain to the woman that I had made a terrible mistake—HOWEVER, G was actually alive and well, and comfortably curled up on a chair in a colourful dress! She asked me to handle the enquiry, and to explain to the woman that she wouldn't come out to see her. I was still trying to adjust to the happy puzzle that G was really alive—but then the music faded and so did the vision of G…

This was so real that I awoke perplexed. I have since learned that such 'confusion dreams' are par for the course when one's wits are working overtime to integrate death's strangely altered reality. How many millions of lines of emotional code must one's brain have to re-write in order to account for the conundrum that one's dearly beloved has become unseen—especially when we were privileged to have a 24/7 union, unlike so many who rarely even have the luxury of a whole weekend together. Was there a specific message in this dream? I took it to say that even if people from a long time ago were still looking for G, she was saying to me, "I trust you to handle everything."

The setting of another dream harked back to 30 years before. I realised that it was recalling a time when I was in the midst of a divorce, while at the same time endeavouring to raise myself up by my bootstraps in a whole new industry. Wasn't the subconscious telling me, via this dream, that the same situation was now being faced, albeit on a different level: I'm within a greater grief zone (it is said that the distress caused by divorce is second only to that of a loved one's death) and yet I am learning, by hard work, the skills needed to operate without my best mate?

Ten days after her passing, I was in the middle of a poignant dream where I was helping G physically around the house—when I was abruptly awoken by the clock-radio switching on. It was playing the Australian folk tune *True Blue*. The message? I'm still helping G by all that I'm doing post-her-decease. I could feel sad and 'truly blue' about it all, or I could simply switch focus and recognise her 'true blue' quality.

* * *

G and I shared the conviction that people's paths in life are guided by a Providential Force of compassionately wise proportions, which could be trusted with our every circumstance. That is probably why G continued to epitomise buoyancy in the face of the grim medical diagnoses and treatments.

"There's a bigger picture at work here. We may not understand it or know where it's going, but let's trust the fact that everything is working for the best... That's our faith." This was the kind of approach which we shared. It is said that some people view the spiritual life as they would a cold shower. It might be good for their health but they are glad when it's over, whereas for G, the spiritual life was as natural to her as was water to a fish. To paraphrase Wordsworth, she could indeed *tread life's common way in cheerful Godliness.*

As a result, the time in the crowded hospital waiting rooms, where so many people bravely nursed their daunting medical prospects, followed by yet more hours of treatment where the staff's unusual joviality belied their patients' sobering prognoses, was endured by G with calm, trusting realism.

Of course, all of this is put to the ultimate test when mortality beckons. Confronted by the sheer profundity and suddenness of her absence, the search for an explanation is not easily settled by the traditional notions about heaven, hell and the hereafter. It is no longer a remote concern but comes down to the very real question, "Where is she?"

I found myself looking for all sorts of explanations in books of philosophy, theology and poetry, or asking thoughtful people for their ideas. Most are either struck mute, or hold firmly to the religious explanations which they have been taught, or offer plausible analogies to calm the agitation of those bereft. "Think of her as having gone on a long journey, where she is savouring new sights and sounds," said someone. When pressed for more details, the person came to the same conclusion as the writer of *The Rubaiyat of Omar Khayyam* (which G often quoted):

> Strange, is it not? that of the myriads who
> Before us pass'd the door of Darkness through
> Not one returns to tell us of the Road,
> Which to discover we must travel too.

About six weeks after G's passing, I felt a strong urge to consult a psychic. I wrote out several questions of the most predictable kind, such as: How is G on the other side? What messages does she have for me and her children? With whom has she most resonated in her new state? I didn't go ahead with it. I am sure that there are good psychics, but I felt that for me it would be adopting a soft option. As I reasoned to myself, isn't it being more honest to trust my instinct that a strong spirit can't be crushed by bodily death?

*   *   *

Dr Raymond Moody's book *Life After Life* (1975) always interested me. He surveyed thousands of people who medically 'died', only to be later revived, often with a remarkably changed attitude to death. A recently-published book includes a 74-year-old psychotherapist's account which echoes many of those recorded in Moody's book. A critical injury which took this woman perilously close to death produced an experience which resulted in her re-thinking her hard-headed rationalism:

> It was an amazing experience, and because of it, I really don't feel afraid of death. It was beautiful. I'm not in a hurry, mind you, but it was such an exquisite experience, such freedom. It was like riding on the

mist; like being a drop of moisture and riding on the mist. The experience demystified death for me. I don't have fear about it now. I'm comfortable.

I am content to accept that G's death has been a liberation for her. This helps assuage the sadness of her not being with me in the way which she always was…

6. Musings

Death lies on her like an untimely frost
Upon the sweetest flower of all the field.
　　　　　　　—W. Shakespeare

IN the early weeks I had to get away from the house at least every second day and have some people contact, even if it meant taking a long walk—as if I could walk off or out-walk my sadness—hoping to run into someone with whom at the very least to exchange a greeting. I would plan ahead in the diary, wondering how I would survive from day one to day three without some interaction, so profound was the loneliness of being completely on my own after loving each and all day with G for so long.

Now that many months have elapsed, this sort of panic feeling has gone. I'm more content with my own company. I concentrate on what has to be done, rather than being focussed on the empty spot left by G.

* * *

Of course, certain poignant moments still crop up unexpectedly. It's time to update my will. I read over the current one in which I left everything to her and it takes me back to the time when it was prepared. It was a procedural duty to be accomplished with little awareness for the day when it would need to be reviewed. Now I would be returning to the same legal office. Last time I was there, I was with her. I would be making my new will with no place for her name, *yet I owe everything to her...*

*   *   *

Colliding with the inexplicability of death in a way equates with supreme simplicity. One minute she's there—the next minute, she's not—and that's that. She's gone. The real mystery, the supreme conundrum, is how I will go on living and whether it will ever bring happiness. For instance, after all these months, her clothes are still in the wardrobe and her bathroom is still replete with her cosmetic accoutrements. It would be a simple matter to remove everything, but at this moment I just don't want to do that. Her personality, her ineffable presence, still lives here—and I'm happy that it does. I don't mean to be overly dramatic. I realise that I'll wake up one morning and just know that it's time to move onto the next stage, when she can continue to be part of the fabric of this house, but that her clothes and things no longer have to be here. Until that day comes, I just want to rest content with things remaining as they've always been.

* * *

I heard a neurosurgeon explaining the importance of sleep to the human brain. Using a computer analogy, he said, "Each night's sleep reboots the brain and de-fragments the hard disk." I am sure that one day scientists will discover that bereavement involves the same sort of 're-booting and de-fragging', though over a much longer time frame.

* * *

There's an attunement to loss in some of the familiar New Testament verses. After the death of Jesus, the disciples said, "Were not our hearts burning within us while he talked with us on the road and opened the Scriptures to us?" (Luke 24:32). How easily I could transpose that to say, "Did not my heart burn within me when G and I talked by the hour, by the day, by the year, by the decade…"

I understand better the words of the Catholic Mass, "Do this in memory of me," when believers are invited to participate in the ritual which remembers all that Jesus has done. So many things I do 'in memory of G': Putting a meal together as she did, tending the garden as she did, responding to mail and enquiries as she would have done, and performing the myriad routine acts that constituted our life together. All of this is done in a 'sacramental' way, as if she's here with me or even living through me.

Perhaps for some people, a new broom sweeps clean, and that's why I'm often asked, "Will you stay in the same house?" It's not out of a morbid duty that I answer, "Yes, of course, for the foreseeable future." Rather it's because this place suited us so well, and still does, even though I'm alone. Some perceptive souls point out the perils. "You walk a tightrope, don't you," observed one, "because the house is so full of reminders of her that it must make it very hard for you…" I would rather live contentedly with the home's memories than flee from them.

* * *

"I know a lady who always talks to her deceased husband," one newly-bereaved woman told me. "Is there something wrong with me because I don't talk to mine?" I am sure that a counsellor would say that it's not a matter of being emotionally correct or incorrect when you are in this territory of loss. I admit that I sometimes have conversations with G and imagine how she would respond to certain situations. Apart from alleviating the loneliness, it is a way of allowing our life together to continue meaning all that it ever meant. "What do you think about this?" or "What do you make of that person?", I might ask her in my mind. She loses none of her grit and verve by being unseen. She would be the last to want to be sentimentalised.

* * *

Someone bounces up and brightly says, "Hi! I haven't seen you for such a long time," and looking around, the person continues, "Where's G?" Is there any easy way of breaking the news? You take the person aside and begin as gently as you can, "G was ill for a while, and then…" At the same time, you're trying to keep yourself in check as you revisit the hurtful sequence all over again.

* * *

It is a testament to G's vitality that for the most part people talked of her passing quite naturally. Among those who knew her well, there was no tiptoeing around her exit to eternity. It is as if her greatness of spirit provided them with a reassurance that she would continue to be in their hearts even if her body had been lost. Of course, there were some who never mentioned my loss of G. I put this down to their embarrassment or awkwardness, especially if they did not really know or understand she-who's-gone.

* * *

Losing a mate certainly affects one's confidence. Even facing the world as a 'community of two' is head and shoulders above having to face it alone. As a twosome, you initiate things together and spark each other along. When alone and bereft, it takes a tremendous effort to get started on anything.

*   *   *

Sometimes during the early months, in the middle of the night, there were momentary feelings almost of *panic*. It was as if a gap had opened up in my life which involved so many empty hours (especially on the weekend) that somehow I would have to fill on my own. At such times, I petulantly felt like demanding that she be returned—that I'd had enough of this game! Of course when the sun rises and the world takes on colour and proportion, and my feet are on the ground, I am reminded that G would expect me to do my very best with each day.

*   *   *

In certain desolate moments, I was conscious of the need to sharpen up my 'self-talk': "If the positions were reversed, and it were you who had died and it was G who was living, would you want her to feel listless and aimless? Of course not! You would expect her to cherish life even more and to make the most of every opportunity and encounter. Please become fully involved in life…"

Admittedly it is often easier to say than do, but I found that when I could stand outside myself and take an external viewpoint, it was easier to step away from the shadows of a downhearted lethargy or a helpless inertia.

* * *

Someone, anxious to offer solace, asked with concern, "Do you have somewhere to go so as to be with her? Do you visit her grave site?"

* * *

Two heads are better than one was a resounding dictum of our life together. "I'd like your help with the next sentence," G might say. "What are you wanting to say?" I would reply—and very quickly we would have the message all worked out. This is how it was with almost every discussion or decision. She could pick up where I left off and vice versa. I appreciated the invaluability of this when she was alive. I'm acutely aware of its absence now.

* * *

"She was the cleverest woman I ever met," said one long-time acquaintance. "She was always helpful. It was a pleasure to know her, and a privilege to be known by her." A speech like that, coming six months down the track, unsurprisingly brings a catch to the voice as I try to reply.

* * *

Just when you feel that you've got everything worked out—your world view is getting back to normal, you feel confident that you're close to restoring even keel, yes, you're quite sure that you'll manage OK—just then, the chasm yawns before you, with the terrible realization, "I'll never see G again." The lump rises in the throat, the prick of tears hits the back of the eyes, and you stare abstractedly into the middle distance, momentarily struck dumb as you confront the vast impenetrable mystery of death. No wonder G's daughter says that it is still simply too painful to think of her as gone, and holds to the idea of her being on that long holiday. One's poor mind can only cope with so much…

* * *

No matter how much I go out (in the earliest weeks, it was to escape), what awaits me on return is an empty apartment. It is not a particularly large one but it's still room after room where it is only me. I would still cling to our little intimacies, and call out as I opened the front door, "I'm home," and imagine that I would glimpse her giving her little wave from the bed, as she raised her head to smile and say, "Come and tell me all the news…"

∗ ∗ ∗

It is just over five months since the fateful day and I happened to ring G's daughter on the mobile phone that G and I shared. Her daughter replied, "It's funny. I know that it's you calling, but Mum's name came up on my phone. I'm going to leave it like that. It's a comfort…"

∗ ∗ ∗

Even if I am out on an errand, I'll do what has to be done, then hurry home—but why hurry home when all that awaited me was an empty abode? On the other hand, I couldn't abide the thought of prolonged aimless sauntering, trying to manufacture some contentment when the only real joy came from having someone like G at your side to share the outing and conversation. Being solo in a crowd seems to magnify rather than diminish the sense of loss. On one such outing, I impulsively bought a second-hand book. Isn't it strange that I would feel immediately better with a book in hand, and not so 'alone-ly'.

∗ ∗ ∗

Even doing a functional task such as sorting receipts for the bookkeeping set off the hidden little sorrow-detonations. The places and dates on the receipts recreated the very 'wheres and whens' of our togetherness before she went.

* * *

Yet again, I am reminded that one of the most profound markers of bereavement is the 'first time syndrome'. On the one hand there's the reluctance to visit so-and-so spot because it's most closely associated with her. On the other hand, there is the excruciating awkwardness of being somewhere where she should be. We were a team. If either of us were absent or late for whatever reason, the immediate question from the person we were due to meet would be, "Where is G?" or "Where is he?" Now it's just me. The dynamics of the relationship are all changed. There's just one of us when there should be two.

* * *

You take your 'sentimental little journeys' on a quiet Sunday morning when there are few around. You take a familiar path and recall snatches of conversation along the way… her comment about a particular building or plant or a view, the story that she told here, the reminiscence that occurred to her there. Am I torturing myself to do this? I feel that it's honouring her. I'd rather experience it, than avoid it or drown it or crowd it out.

Somehow, it siphons off yet one more eyedropper of sadness.

* * *

Some of the people whom I've engaged in conversation at bus stops and on the buses during those first weeks will never know that their willingness to exchange a few words with a stranger was like a lifebuoy to someone cast adrift in a sea of loneliness, who was treading water with the bottom way out of reach.

* * *

Grieving sometimes seems to slow life to walking pace, when you're conscious not only of the chimes of the hour, but the very tick of the clock.

* * *

Why am I so mindful, at the most obscure moments, about my loss of G? I suppose two people who are so close are connected by myriad power cords, more likely millions than dozens. When death wrenches away the beloved, it feels as if the survivor is left with all of these minute cords just dangling. I suppose this explains the incredible tiredness, because there's no longer a closed power circuit. Each of those loose cords has to be re-plugged somewhere else. How long does that take? What if no new source can be found? That means a particular circuit becomes inoperative, or the cord has to be re-engineered to find a new source within oneself. I suppose that's what is meant when some people eventually 'come back to life' a year or so after losing their mate. They've established new energy sources within themselves, and have far fewer 'dangling cables' or 'loose strings' needing to be tied up.

*   *   *

It's a Sunday. I've performed the usual domestic chores and there's even a little more warmth in the sun than usual, as if the promise of spring is in the air—but even then, there's the poignant stab, recalling the really important element that's missing from this scene: she's not here. It's not only songs such as, *I'll be seein' you in all the old familiar places* which press the button. Even the subtleties of the weather contain reminders of she-who-is-so-dearly-missed.

*   *   *

I asked their mother whether G's young grandchildren speak about her. The younger one is too young, she said, but the eight-year-old still gets upset when his mother reads him a book that G had inscribed in beautiful calligraphy, news which makes me swallow hard.

*   *   *

A newspaper article talks about the grief that returns long after the event, often when you least expect it. The writer calls it the "second wave of sorrow". Unexpectedly, after seeing a sad film, the writer found himself weeping quietly at the back of the bus. "At the time of his death, I was organised and in control. I had to be," he said. "The first wave of grief was manageable and contained, but this wave, the second wave, came from nowhere and swamped me."

*   *   *

An email arrives relating to an enquiry that G made years ago in connection with her family tree. Once more the canyon of her physical absence opens yawningly wide. 'How interested she'd be in all of this,' is the poignant reaction. "But hold on," I query myself, "why am I still thinking about continuing the research into her family tree if she's no longer here?" I decide that I'll continue with the historical fieldwork because as part of the ever-present backdrop (front-drop?) of my life, G continues to be here. At the very least, her grandchildren may treasure her family's story one day, just as they'll cherish their memory of her.

*   *   *

The aim of life is to have a substratum of joy—but at the moment, my substratum feels melancholic. If you have the former, it affects all that takes place on the surface level of your life; if the latter, then there's a dulling or diminishing influence. I'm sure that bereavement is all about gradually converting the melancholia to joy.

*   *   *

It hits you freshly all over again. You stare at her photo, and for the life of you, it just can't be fathomed that she's not here, and she just won't appear from around the corner. Maybe the day has something to do with it. It feels like summer has begun, and what goes with summer but G—but where is she? Just when you think you're past tears, here they come again—another squall out of a bright blue sky. I suppose that the seeds were planted this morning. A fellow who lived in this building a long time ago was lamenting G's passing. "No matter what the situation, she was always bright and happy," he reminisced. Those words went straight through to the heart, summoning up her loss all over again. Returning home to the apartment's crowding emptiness which is full of G, I know it's predictable, but again I just shake my head and silently say, "I still just can't believe she's not here…"

Isn't the mind protective… It's going to let me down gently, and continue to permit a part of me to think that she's still here somewhere, albeit 'semi-physically'. If the mind worked the other way and just 'deleted' the G file, it would surely kill me.

*   *   *

Ironically, I have more time on my hands now because caring for G, especially in her last six months, absorbed every effort. On the other hand, even though she was very ill, the psychic impetus which she supplied meant that things got done with energy. These days it takes much more effort to work on 'sole power'. Often it feels as if I'm trying to start a cold engine. At other times, just when I manage to be moving along nicely, suddenly the wind goes out of the sails and I feel on the verge of becalmment in the emotional doldrums.

*   *   *

It's surely a fortuity that several weeks ago I was invited to take up a totally new pastime—crewing on a sailing yacht. Quite apart from the joy of making new acquaintances and 'learning the ropes' from scratch, it's proving to be both a literal and metaphorical way of putting new wind in my sails.

*   *   *

I've just returned from a shopping outing with cousin L. It's the first time back to that centre without G. The cousin talked about what G bought at various shops, and she recalled that G had looked tired. I felt like stamping my foot and saying crossly to the Powers-that-be, "Where is G? She should have been there with us.

She should be here right now!" Again I shake my head and say for the nth time: "I just can't believe that she's gone forever." Why not turn back time? It's a beautiful day. The birds are singing, the grass is resplendently green, the sunshine is sparkling—and all that's missing is her.

Strangely enough, Providence's impeccable timing means that this reverie is interrupted by the arrival of a heartfelt condolence message from someone who's been out of touch for a while. At that moment, I don't feel so alone in missing her…

* * *

Yesterday's visit to a local outdoor concert was a measure of how far I had come in these months. This time I felt no reluctance about speaking to people. The pall of sadness had lifted. I remembered how I had felt months before when I was in two minds about running into people who might recognize me, because I had no wish to speak to anyone. I would take my walks at times of the day to avoid contact. By contrast, now I feel more confident speaking about G. It's nice to be able to record this improvement. A large portion of the healing feels as if it has taken place.

Epilogue

My sun sets to rise again.
— Robert Browning

IN the months since G's passing, I would like to think that I am past the sting of tears, but I have said that before and they have always returned. Yes, there still arise those stark perceptions of loss—yet I pause at that point: a spirit like hers will never succumb to nothingness.

G's wish to be cremated was in keeping with her idea that death permits the freeing of one's spirit. Her ashes have not yet been 'broadcast'. I could say 'distributed' but broadcast is nicely in keeping with her respect for the disseminating power of the printed word. I've made a list of spots which were close to her heart where her ashes could nourish the soil. One day, it will be the right time to have each handful ceremonially laid to rest.

In the absence of a gravestone, this memoir could well be a fitting memorial for her. As for an epitaph, I am sure that she would agree to taking a leaf out of

Leigh Hunt's book, and accept, from his poem below (one that she frequently quoted), the line which adorns his gravestone:

Write me as one that loves his fellow-men

* * *

Abou Ben Adhem

by Leigh Hunt

Abou Ben Adhem (may his tribe increase!)
Awoke one night from a deep dream of peace
And saw within the moonlight in his room,
Making it rich and like a lily in bloom,
An angel writing in a book of gold.
Exceeding peace had made Ben Adhem bold,
And to the presence in the room he said,
"What writest thou?" The vision raised its head,
And, with a look made of all sweet accord,
Answered, "The names of those who love the Lord."
"And is mine one?" said Abou. "Nay, not so,"
Replied the angel. Abou spoke more low,
But cheerly still; and said, "I pray thee, then,
Write me as one that loves his fellow-men."
The angel wrote, and vanished. The next night
It came again with a great wakening light,
And showed the names whom love of God had blessed,
And lo! Ben Adhem's name led all the rest!

Appendix

There's a divinity that shapes our ends,
Rough-hew them how we will.

— Shakespeare

WHO can say that one death is any 'better' than another for those who are left behind. The sudden passing of one's spouse is possibly the most devastating, and yet the account below—written in response to reading this memoir—is a reminder that the seismic emotional shocks produced by a loved one's loss can continue rippling through one's inner world, no matter how different the circumstances.

Remembering

READING Gerard's memoir I was left with the feeling of how similar and yet so different our experiences of loss can be. For my part, that question of what to do with the clothes and shoes—the symbols of our loved one's presence—that were now left unused in the wardrobe brought up the same sort of issues as related by Gerard. I was eventually able to give away his lovely shoes but I kept the ones he liked most for a long time. Although he hadn't worn them for years because of his illness I simply left them in their usual place. I know someone who 10 years later still had her husband's jumpers stacked in the wardrobe as he had left them. That first time someone asks you how your love is and you have to say they are now not with you —that same awkwardness is probably experienced by many. Those moments when you think you are going mad because of some irrational behaviour or feeling, I think will be common emotions.

The very big difference for me however related to my feelings and actions when my love died. It was not a time of being calm and loving as I know others have experienced. My feelings were of panic and absolute coldness. This is my story of the worst half hour of my life.

That morning I came into the hospital as I had done for the last three weeks. My two step-children and I kept a vigil around his bedside but this morning was different—it was my birthday and tomorrow would be my step-daughter's birthday. I arrived with a mission, to tell my love that he had to leave us today because he couldn't go tomorrow—this would be too hard on A. From my years of studying history, I knew that a story could always be turned round to produce a positive outcome. I had convinced myself of the positive story I was going to create on this particular morning. I was strong, wasn't I?

The necessary words were said. I asked that he give me one last birthday present—to relieve us all of the torment of his struggle to stay alive. For years he had fought with amazing strength to stay alive but the time had now come. I will never forget my last words to him on that morning, "My darling, you must leave us."

Within moments of my saying these words, my step-son arrived. S sat down with his father and I left the room saying that I would be back soon. I did not even say goodbye to my love—but I know that those 10 minutes S had with his father would have been lovely for them both. Their relationship had not been easy and I feel that they made their peace with each other that morning.

When S came to tell me his father had gone I hugged him and we both went back to the hospital room. Although 10 minutes previously I had seen my love as he was, just skin and bones, I did not think anything of it. Now, I looked down and saw, in cold-hearted detail, the face and body that did not belong to my love. He was not there for me. I felt nothing except that I wanted to run away from this scene. I was very grateful that S was with me that day because he did whatever needed to be done.

Once out of the hospital room my heart began to beat frantically as though in a panic. I wanted to run but somehow couldn't—and then, ever so slowly, it seemed my heart began to freeze over. It was as though a hand was pushing down on my heart almost to the extent of hurting me. I look back now and realise that it was probably at that moment, still in the corridor of the hospital, that my heart almost broke.

I kept saying to myself that I was strong and that this was the best thing for my love and myself. He could rest in peace at long last and I could get on with my life. It took me two years before I saw a counsellor and then slowly my heart began to heal.

It was not until I talked with a friend who had felt similar emotions to mine, when her beloved mother died, that I realised that this response to losing a love was not cowardly or unloving. It was part of the varied nature of what makes us human. I will be grateful if by sharing these thoughts others may be helped to overcome the loss of a beloved.

NOTES

p. vi – Rabindranath Tagore (1861-1941).

p. 1 – Johann Wolfgang von Goethe (1749-1832), Conversations with Eckermann, May 2, 1824.

p. 13 – Dylan Thomas (1914–53), "Do not go gentle into that good night" (1951).

p. 15 – Adam Lindsay Gordon (1833-70), "Ye Wearie Wayfarer".

p. 16 – A.E. Housman (1859-1936), *A Shropshire Lad*, Palmer's Press, Ludlow, 1987, XXXI, p. 46.

p. 18 – W.H. Auden (1907-73), "Stop all the clocks, cut off the telephone".

p. 21 – W. Shakespeare (1564-1616), *King Lear*, Act 5, Scene III.

p. 26 – A. Price Hughes & Mary Lee Hall, "Turn Again To Life" (source unknown).

p. 37 – A.W. Pinero (1855-1934).

p. 40 – William Wordsworth (1770–1850), "England, 1802".

p. 41 – Edward FitzGerald (1809-83), *The Rubaiyat of Omar Khayyam* (1859).

p. 42 – Raymond Moody (b. 1944), *Life After Life*, Bantam, New York, 1975.

p. 42 – H. & S. Stone, (Editing & Reflections by Dianne Braden), *The Fireside Chats with Hal and Sidra Stone*, Delos Publications, 2011.

p. 44 – W. Shakespeare (1564-1616), *Romeo & Juliet*, Act 4, Scene V.

p. 56 – Steven Ogden, "A Second Wave of Sorrow", *Courier Mail*, 11 August 2011, p. 31.

p. 60 – Robert Browning (1812-1889), "At The 'Mermaid'".

p. 61 – J.H. Leigh Hunt (1784-1859), "Abou Ben Adhem".

p. 62 – W. Shakespeare, *Hamlet*, Act 5, Scene II.

ACKNOWLEDGEMENTS

THE AUTHOR wishes to thank Jeanelle Bergin for her encouragement which helped this book to see the light of day. Sincere gratitude for their considered feedback is also offered to Jo Glasson, Mary Hockaday and Kay Fraser (as well as for 'Remembering' in the Appendix), and to Andrea Pullar for her careful proofreading and cogent suggestions.